HIDE AND SEEK

Mona Gansberg Hodgson

Illustrated by Chris Sharp

CPH
SAINT LOUIS

To my mother June Gansberg–Jensen
for her devotion in raising me in the way I should go.
With special thanks to my editors at CPH
and to Elisabeth Brown Hendricks
for their help in editing this book.

Scripture quotations are taken from the HOLY BIBLE, NEW INTERNATIONAL VERSION®. NIV®. Copyright © 1973, 1978, 1984 by International Bible Society. Used by permission of Zondervan Publishing House. All rights reserved.

Text copyright © 2000 Mona Gansberg Hodgson
Illustrations copyright © 2000 Concordia Publishing House
Published by Concordia Publishing House
3558 S. Jefferson Avenue, St. Louis, MO 63118-3968
Manufactured in the United States of America

1   2   3   4   5   6   7   8   9   10   09   08   07   06   05   04   03   02   01   00

WHAT'S INSIDE

Note to Adults

Hide and Seek can be used in a variety of settings as family devotions or in a child's personal, quiet time with the Lord. These devotions are easily adapted for use in the home, school, or church classroom.

In this nine-week study on the fruit of the Spirit, children will discover that learning about God and His ways can be fun. They'll come away from each devotion with practical tips on how to apply biblical truths to their personal faith life.

While helping to develop reading and reasoning skills, the stories and activities will also help children seek out hidden truths that lead them to discover how the Holy Spirit helps their faith grow so their lives can produce abundant fruit—the fruit of the Spirit. Each devotion features several components with child-compelling and spiritually significant symbols to support a perspective of exploration and discovery.

The devotions are designed for a child to spend a full week exploring each fruit of the Spirit. If the child begins on Sunday and is consistent each day, he or she will end on Saturday with a "Something to Do" activity. However, the devotions are not numbered or named for the days of the week. The child may begin on any day and continue as works best.

Each devotion begins with a simple explanation of the featured fruit of the Spirit. Thereafter, children will dive into the theme with a fun desert critter anecdote. Check out the library or bookstores for books that teach more about the featured desert critters. Prayer suggestions are offered for each day, encouraging the development of a deeper and more personal prayer life.

A lively retelling of a companion Bible story is also featured. Consider reading the complete story from the Bible as a family.

Throughout the week's study, the child will be encouraged to interact with biblical truths through a journal and other activities that reinforce the lesson. Depending on the age of the child, you might offer your help with the completion of these activities. Simpler puzzles are offered for younger children with more complicated ones for the older reader.

A key verse will encourage the child to memorize Scripture that supports each fruit of the Spirit. Offer your help as needed. When a verse can be recited from memory, the child is invited to color the featured critter on the map found on page 10. Help your child learn all of the key verses and fill the map with critters.

Mona Gansberg Hodgson

Note to Kids

Hi there!

    I live in the desert of Arizona and I wrote this book for you. Do you know who made the desert? Genesis 1:1 says, *"God created the heavens and the earth."* God made everything, and that includes the desert and its critters.

    We are going to explore the desert. As we go exploring, we'll discover some exciting things about God. Every chapter in this book has something fun for each day of the week.

    I'm sure there are a lot of things you would like to have. Do you know what God wants you to have more than anything else? He wants you to have trust in His promises for the sake of Jesus Christ.

    God the Father sent His Son Jesus to be our Savior from sin. Do you know what sin is? Sin means that there is something wrong with us that makes us do things to disobey God. We sin when we do things like stealing, cheating, lying, or hurting others. We can also sin by not doing things we know we should. For example, we sin when we do not share what we have or help someone that is hurt.

God still loves us when we sin, but He does not love the sins we do. That's why Jesus came as a baby at Christmas, died on the cross for our sins, and rose again from the dead—so that He could take the punishment for our sin. That's what we believe. That's called faith.

The ways we show our faith and share God's love are called the *Fruit of the Spirit*. In John 15:14 and 16 Jesus says, *"You are My friends … You did not choose Me, but I chose you to go and bear fruit—fruit that will last."* This kind of fruit is not like oranges, or apples, or bananas. The fruit of the Spirit doesn't grow on trees. Instead, it grows out of faith in Jesus, God's Son. The Holy Spirit helps our faith in Christ Jesus to grow in our hearts so that we can show others what it's like to trust, depend, and rely on God's love.

Turn the page to find out how you can discover more about the fruit of the Spirit. Come exploring with me. It will be our own kind of hide and seek!

Mona Gansberg Hodgson

How to Use This Book

The stories and activities in these chapters will help you learn what God teaches about the fruit of the Spirit. Here is a guide to your critter exploration and Bible discovery.

Fruit of the Spirit: Your body needs water to stay alive and to grow. Whenever we hear God's Word and stories about His steadfast love, our faith grows so that it can produce the fruit of the Spirit.

A Better View: Have you ever tried to see something that was far away? Binoculars (ben–ok–u–lars) have special lenses that bring things into focus that are far away. This part of the devotion will help you understand the fruit of the Spirit and bring it into focus.

You Can Pray: Hikers carry a compass so it can point north and show them which way to go. Prayer is like a compass because it points to the cross. We can find God's direction for us when we pray.

Detective Time: Look for the magnifying glass to find puzzles for you to solve or figure out so that you can learn more about God's love.

A Bible Story to Read: You might use a backpack to take  along the things you need when you go to school or to your grandma's house. This backpack will help you remember that you can take Bible stories and God's promises with you wherever you go.

A Verse to Learn: Maps show you how to get to where you  are going. The Bible does that too! It shows us God's plan for our salvation, and teaches us that our way to heaven is through Jesus, who first brought God's love from heaven to us.

My Journal: A saguaro cactus is one of the many cacti that  can be found in most of the deserts in Arizona. This section will give you a chance to write or draw pictures about the things you are discovering.

Something to Do: A lot of desert critters—like skunks, rats, and bunnies—use their feet to get things done. Here you will find ideas for things you can do to show the fruit of the Spirit and share God's love with others.

Critter Map

Circle each critter as you learn the key Bible verse in each chapter.

The Fruit of the Spirit

The fruit of the Spirit is love, joy, peace, patience, kindness, goodness, faithfulness, gentleness and self-control. (Galatians 5:22–23)

LOVE

A Better View

Do you know what it means to love someone? When you love others, you care about them and want to be there to help and serve them. You show that you care when you talk to someone that no one else seems to like. Or when you help your friend study for a hard test. And you show that you care when you ask "What's wrong?" when someone looks sad.

In John 13:34, Jesus said, *"As I have loved you, so you must love one another."* God wants us to love others the way He loves us. We cannot show God's love to others by ourselves. God helps us share His love to others.

Duck, Duck, Quail

Lots of different desert
critters live all around me.
Quail are some of those critters.

Do you know what a quail is? It's a desert bird with a feathery top-knot on its head. Quail look a little bit like pears with legs, feet, and tail feathers.

Quail arrive every year around March when the weather gets warmer. We see male and female quail run across our roads. We notice them playing follow-the-leader over the rocks in our front yard. Then we find them in our backyard, marching as in a parade across the top of our chain-link fence.

Quail like to hide, rest, and nest
in the mesquite (mes–keet) bushes and
sagebrush behind our house. Each morning and evening
we can hear their strange call. Quail don't tweet or chirp like
some birds. Their call is three notes. The middle note is the
highest and loudest—"Yoo–HOO–hoo."

The mother and father quail like to bring their families into
our backyard to show off their babies. They poke through the
holes in our chain-link fence, or they scurry under the fence
through holes that cottontail rabbits dig.

Have you ever seen baby quail? They look like hairy
walnuts with legs when they come for their first visit.

After they've grown a little, they look like tennis balls with legs and feet. It's a lot of fun to watch them wobble and wander.

One day it looked like the quail family was playing a game. Nine babies wandered around, pecking grass seeds. Suddenly, they all quit snacking and ducked down into the grass. Why do you think they did that?

I kept watching through my screen door. The feathered family started snacking again, but soon the father quail called out the three notes. Again, the babies ducked down into the bunches of grass and froze like statues. Their father had given them a warning.

Maybe the father quail had seen or heard a cat prowling around. Or maybe he had spotted a hawk or a raven flying close by. The father knew there was danger and he gave a signal to his family. The babies stayed hidden until their father called out again. The father quail watched over his children. His love and care for them kept them safe.

God our heavenly Father is always watching over us. And He is our Creator and He wants what is best for us. He has given us a family to love and care for us. He sent Jesus to be our Savior from sin. He gave us the Bible so that we can learn more about Him. He even gave us prayer so we can talk to Him. And He promises to listen when we pray. That is love!

God loves us even more than the father quail cares about his fuzzy babies. I like knowing that God loves me. Don't you?

You Can Pray

Thank God for loving you.
Think about the people God has put
in your life who take care of you.
Thank God for them.

Detective Time

Can you count? How many quail can you find in this picture?
Color the picture using your favorite colors.

Detective Time

God created the heavens and the earth. That includes the desert. God put lots of plants and critters in the desert. Put the letters of each word in the right order. Then you will discover the names of some desert plants and critters.

Write the unscrambled words on the lines below. Use the answer key in the back of the book to check your answers.

uqali _____

miesqtue _____

btabrsi _____

husragseb _____

wkha _____

venra _____

ctucas _____

You Can Pray

Thank God for creating you.
There is no one else like you!
And thank Him for creating quail
and all other critters.

A Bible Story to Read

Ruth
1:1-17

Have you ever heard of Naomi and Ruth?

Naomi lived with her husband and two sons in Judah. When there was a shortage of food in Judah, Naomi and her family moved to Moab. Then Naomi's husband died.

Naomi's sons married women who lived in Moab. One son married a woman named Ruth. Another son married Orpah. The sons and their wives took care of Naomi. After 10 years, her sons died too.

Naomi was poor, and she missed her husband and her sons. But God was still watching over her. He had a special plan for Naomi.

One day Naomi heard that there was food in her homeland once again. She and her daughters-in-law decided to move to Judah.

While they were on their way, Naomi stopped and told Ruth and Orpah to return home to live with their mothers.

Ruth and Orpah cried when Naomi kissed them good-bye. Orpah left to go back to Moab. What do you think Ruth did?

The Bible says that Ruth chose to go with Naomi to the land of Judah.

Ruth told Naomi, *"Where you go I will go, and where you stay I will stay. Your people will be my people and your God my God"* (Ruth 1:16b).

God used Naomi to teach Ruth to love Him. God helped Ruth serve and take care of Naomi. God used Ruth to remind Naomi that He loved and cared for her.

Love is a fruit of the Spirit. The Holy Spirit helps us know that God loves us and learn how He wants us to love others.

(You can keep reading the book of Ruth to discover other ways God showed Naomi and Ruth that He loved them.)

You Can Pray

Thank God for the example of Ruth. And ask Him to help you learn how to share His love with others.

Detective Time

Ruth showed God's love to Naomi when she left her family and
home in Moab. Can you help Naomi and Ruth find their way to Judah?

Detective Time

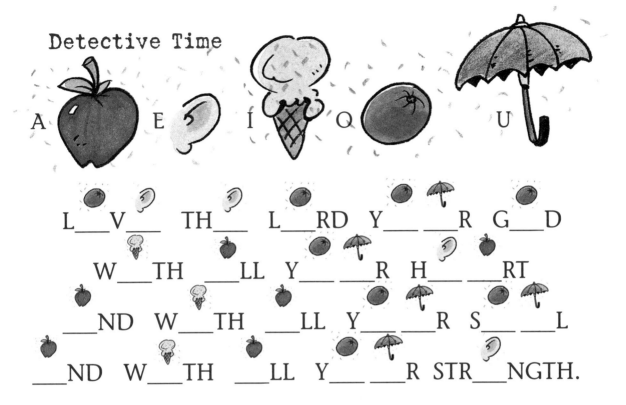

A (apple)　E (bean)　I (ice cream cone)　O (orange)　U (umbrella)

L__V__ TH__ L__RD Y____R G__D

W__TH __LL Y____R H____RT

__ND W__TH __LL Y____R S____L

__ND W__TH __LL Y____R STR__NGTH.

Use the picture clues to fill in the vowels in this Bible verse.
Read Deuteronomy 6:5 to check your answer.

You Can Pray

Ask God to help you learn to trust
in His love more. Thank Him for sending
Jesus to show us the best example of love when
He died and rose again for our salvation.

A Verse to Learn

As I have loved you, so you must love one another.
(John 13:34b)

God wants us to love other people like He has loved us. But loving others as God has loved us means that we are to love everyone, even those who are hard to love. After all, God loves us and forgives us even though we are sinners. He even loves and forgives us when we act like we don't love Him. When we serve the unlovable we are sharing the love God has shown us through Jesus.

John 13:34b

Read the Bible verse again. Can you say the verse without looking at it? When you can say the whole verse without looking at it, repeat it for someone in your family.

When you've said the verse to someone without looking at it, circle the quail on the Critter Map, page 10.

You Can Pray

Think about the people God has put in your life. Your family. Your friends. Your neighbors. Kids at church. Kids at school. Ask God to help you love them and forgive them as Jesus loves and forgives us.

My Journal

In John 15:17, Jesus says, *"This is My command: Love each other."*

A command is something we are supposed to do. In this verse, Jesus tells us to love others. It is something He wants us to do.

Can you think of someone who needs to know about God's love? Write that person's name here. Then write ways that you can show God's love. Or draw a picture of something you can do to show that you care.

You Can Pray

Thank God for the person you wrote about in your journal. Ask God to help you show love to them even when they are unlovable. Ask God to help you tell how God loves everyone through Jesus.

Something to Do

Think of someone you know who is sick. It might be someone in your family or school. It might be a neighbor or someone in your church. Make a get well card. You can use paper and fun stuff to make the card by hand, or you can have someone help you make it on a computer.

Remember to add a note about God's love!

You Can Pray

Thank God for showing His love to you through Jesus. Ask Him to help you show His love by serving others.

A Better View

Day
1

Do you know what joy is?
Joy is a deep gladness.
You might be filled with joy
at Christmas. Or you might feel joy
when you see a friend you haven't
seen in a long time.

The Bible tells about times when
people expressed their joy by
celebrating. Can you think of
things you like to celebrate? I can.

God created us and He loves us.
He sent His Son Jesus as our Savior,
and He forgives our sins. We can
talk to Him through prayer.
That's a lot to celebrate!

LIZARD EXERCISES

Can you guess which desert critter wears scales and eats bugs? If you said a lizard, you're right.

God created thousands of different kinds of lizards. They live in all sorts of places, except where it gets really cold. Lots of lizards like living in the Arizona desert. Can you guess why?

Lizards are reptiles and they are cold-blooded. Do you know what that means? That means their bodies need warm surroundings to make their blood warm enough for their bodies to survive. This is why most lizards live in places with warm weather, like the desert.

Lizards enjoy scurrying around my garage collecting crickets. They like racing across the brick planter around my rose bushes. The scaly critters also like resting in the shade of the flower pots on my patio.

Have you ever seen a lizard doing its exercises? I've never seen a lizard do jumping jacks or sit-ups. But one day while I was in my backyard, I saw a lizard doing push-ups. I'm not joking!

He used his legs to lift his body off the ground and up into the air. Then back down. Then up. Then down again. Why do you think he did that?

The lizard might have been doing push-ups because he wanted to exercise his leg muscles. Or maybe his tummy was getting hot. Pushing up off the patio would help him cool off his tummy. But I think there's another reason for the push-ups.

If I were a lizard, I'd be glad for the sunshine
God sent to warm my body so it
would work right. The push-ups
might be a way for the lizard
to show that he was glad
for God's sunshine.

I want to be like a
lizard. Don't you?
I want to show God
my joy and thanks
for all of the good
things He has done
for me—especially
for sending Jesus,
God's Son-shine,
to fill my heart with the light of His love.

 ## You Can Pray

Thank God for the sunshine He sends to make you warm
and help things grow. Then thank Him for sending
His Son to shine His love on you.

Detective Time

What desert critter reminds us to exercise our joy?

_____

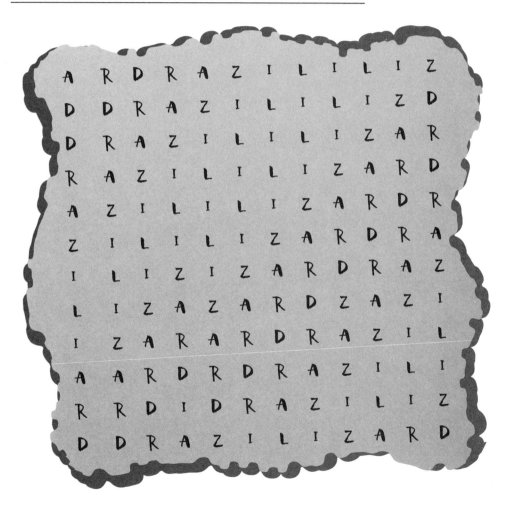

```
A  R  D  R  A  Z  I  L  I  L  I  Z
D  D  R  A  Z  I  L  I  L  I  Z  D
D  R  A  Z  I  L  I  L  I  Z  A  R
R  A  Z  I  L  I  L  I  Z  A  R  D
A  Z  I  L  I  L  I  Z  A  R  D  R
Z  I  L  I  L  I  Z  A  R  D  R  A
I  L  I  Z  I  Z  A  R  D  R  A  Z
L  I  Z  A  Z  A  R  D  Z  A  Z  I
I  Z  A  R  A  R  D  R  A  Z  I  L
A  A  R  D  R  D  R  A  Z  I  L  I
R  R  D  I  D  R  A  Z  I  L  I  Z
D  D  R  A  Z  I  L  I  Z  A  R  D
```

Look at the puzzle above. How many times can you find this critter's name?
Look up, down, forward, and backward!

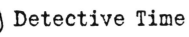

Detective Time

God created us. He made lizards too. What do you know about lizards? Read these sentences and fill in the blanks.

Hint: The answers are in the story.

Lizards are ___ ___ ___ ___ ___ ___ ___ ___.

Lizards wear ___ ___ ___ ___ ___ ___.

Lizards eat ___ ___ ___ ___.

Lizards are ___ ___ ___ ___ — ___ ___ ___ ___ ___ ___ ___.

Lizards like ___ ___ ___ ___ weather best.

Lots of lizards live in the warm ___ ___ ___ ___ ___ ___.

Lizards do ___ ___ ___ ___ — ___ ___ ___.

You Can Pray

Thank God for creating you and for creating lizards.
And thank Him for giving you joy and for sending Jesus,
His Son-shine, to be our Savior from sin.

Nehemiah
12:27-43

A Bible Story to Read

Have you ever heard of Nehemiah?

Nehemiah wasn't a fireman, or a doctor, or a teacher. He worked as a cupbearer for the Emperor of Persia. An emperor is a king. It was part of Nehemiah's job to taste the king's drink to make sure no one had put poison in it. I don't think I'd want that job!

Nehemiah lived in a place troubled by wars. They didn't have jet planes to patrol the area looking for their enemies. They built walls around their cities to guard them.

The Israelites were God's chosen people but they sinned against God by worshiping other gods. God punished them. He let the people of Babylon win a war against Jerusalem. The walls of the city were destroyed. The Israelites had to leave Jerusalem and live in Babylon. Then the Emperor of Persia became the ruler over Babylon.

Nehemiah cared about the Israelites and he wanted to help them. He prayed to God every day and every night. He asked God to show him how to help the Israelites.

Nehemiah went to his king. He asked the king to send him to the land of Judah. He wanted to build a new wall around the city of Jerusalem where his fathers were buried. Nehemiah was full of joy when the king let him go to Jerusalem.

God used Nehemiah to show His people that He forgave them for their sins and still loved them. God also used Nehemiah to help the Israelites build a new wall around Jerusalem.

The Bible says that God's people came together to celebrate when the wall was finished. The Israelites used music to celebrate their joy. They sang songs and played instruments in praise for what God had done for them.

I want to show God my joy for His forgiveness and love too. Don't you? I want to celebrate my joy in many different ways. I want to use my hands, my feet, and my lips as instruments of joy.

Joy is a fruit of the Spirit.
The Holy Spirit will help us have joy.
He will also help us learn how
to share our joy with others.

(You can keep reading the book of Nehemiah to discover the other ways God used Nehemiah to help the Israelites.)

You Can Pray

Thank God for the example of Nehemiah.
Ask Him to help you feel joy. And ask God to help you trust in His promises of love and forgiveness.

Detective Time

Nehemiah and the Israelites trusted in God. God helped them build a new wall around Jerusalem and He filled them with His joy.

Circle the words that name people and things that appeared in the story about Nehemiah. Look up, down, forward, and backward to find them.

Word Bank:
cup
gates
instruments
Israelites
king
prayer
wall

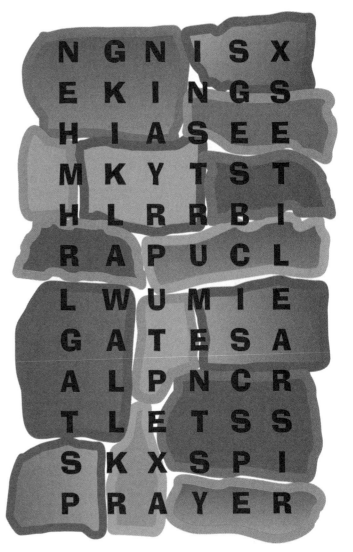

Detective Time

The words on this wall are all mixed up! Unscramble the word on each block. Then write it in the corresponding blank to complete the Bible verse.

#	scrambled
1	A
2	erfhulce
3	ahret
4	si
5	ogod
6	ecimdeni
7	utb
8	a
9	uhdsrce
10	pirsit
11	serid
12	pu
13	het
14	nboes

_____ _____ _____ _____ _____
1   2   3   4   5

_____ , _____ _____ _____ _____
6   7   8   9   10

_____ _____ _____ _____ .
11   12   13   14   Proverbs 17:22

You Can Pray

Feel the joy God gives. Thank Him
for the many things He has done for you.
Remember to thank Him for sending
Jesus as your Savior.

Day
5

A Verse to Learn

The joy of the LORD is your strength.
(Nehemiah 8:10b)

God wants us to feel joy when we think about what He has done for us. Say your name in the verse where you see the word "your." When I do that, the verse reads, "The joy of the Lord is Mona's strength." The love God shows to us through Jesus is stronger than anyone or anything. We are filled with joy when we trust in what the Lord has done for us. He is our strength.

Read the Bible verse again. Can you say the verse without looking at it? When you can say the whole verse without looking at it, repeat it for someone in your family.

Nehemiah 8:10b

When you've said the verse to someone without looking at it, circle the lizard on the Critter Map, page 10.

Thank you!

You Can Pray

Thank God for sending Jesus who showed His love to us on the cross. Ask Him to help you to trust in the strength of His love and to share your joy with others.

My Journal

_____

_____

_____

_____

_____

_____

_____

God sent Jesus to show His love and forgiveness to us.
What other things has God done that give you joy?
Make a list here. On the next page, draw a picture
of something God has given that brings you joy.

You Can Pray

Look at your list or the picture
you drew. Thank God for each of the
things that make you glad.

Something to Do

Psalm 33:3 says,
"Sing to [God] a new song; play skillfully, and shout with joy."

Make up a song about the joy God gives. If you play an instrument, use it in your new song about God. Or look for something in your house that can be used as an instrument: a coffee can for a drum, a cardboard paper towel tube for a horn, or a jar of peppercorns for a tambourine.

You Can Pray

Thank God for the joy He gives.
Ask Him to teach you how to use your voice, your hands, and your feet as instruments of joy to show how you feel because of what God has done for you.

PEACE

A Better View

Do you know what peace is? It's not the same as a piece of candy or a piece of pie. This type of peace is spelled differently and it means something else. Peace is the fruit of the Spirit that comes to us when we know we can trust in God to take care of everything. Peace is the opposite of worry.

You can't have peace and be worried at the same time. In Philippians 4:6–7, the Bible tells us not to worry about anything. It says we should pray about everything. God will help us feel His peace—the kind that will replace the worries.

Grasshopper on Wheels

One morning I backed my Jeep out of the garage. At the end of my driveway, I pulled the shift lever to 'D' for drive. The Jeep jumped forward. That's when I spied a critter clinging to the hood. I took my foot off the gas pedal.

The critter's tiny toes dug into the green paint as she tried to keep from tumbling to the road. She had skinny legs and wings. Can you guess what she was?

If you said she was a grasshopper, you were right! Instead of hopping in blades of grass, the bug-eyed grasshopper stared at the strange-looking windshield wiper blades. The grasshopper was in a very strange place. And she was all alone.

I parked my Jeep on the side of the road. I got out and stared at the shaky grasshopper. Maybe she was cold because she had been blowing in the breeze. Or maybe she was shaky because she was scared.

I thought the grasshopper would hop off the hood, but she didn't move. Maybe she was too afraid, or maybe she was too tired because she was holding on so tight.

I gently scooped her into my hand and lifted her off my hood. Then I put her in the grass. Have you ever seen a grasshopper smile? I think I did.

Do you ever feel alone or afraid? I do. I think we all feel scared sometimes.

Do you know what I do when I feel like a grasshopper on the hood of a moving Jeep? I pray. I might cry first. And I might worry a little bit. But then I remember that I can trust in God to take care of everything. After all, He took care of my biggest problem of all by sending Jesus as my Savior from sin. God gives me His peace.

You Can Pray

Thank God for taking care of you and all of your worries.
Thank Him for sending Jesus so that
your biggest worries called sins can be forgiven.

Detective Time

Find seven grasshoppers in the garage and circle each one. Then color the rest of the picture.

Detective Time

Circle the names of these bug critters that are found in the desert. Look up, down, forward, and backward to find them.

```
S X C R I C K E T S
R B S Y N B Z T A R
E U S M S S S G R U
P G N A T S T N A G
P S O L I V E T N A
O C I R C R K A T T
H O P P K R C N U S
S L R K B X R N L T
S T O C U T C T A I
A B C I G U B R S C
R E S T S T I C M K
G R S S H P P R S S
```

You Can Pray

Thank God for creating you. And thank Him for creating critters.

1 Samuel
17:1-49

A Bible Story to Read

The Bible tells the true story about a boy named David who went to fight a giant.

The Philistine army had gathered for war against the Israelites. Goliath was a Philistine soldier. He was over nine feet, nine inches tall. Most of the really tall NBA basketball players are only seven feet tall. Ceilings in most houses are eight feet high. Extra-high ceilings are usually ten feet high. Goliath was huge!

For 40 days, Goliath came out and shouted to the army of Israel. He said, "Choose a man to fight me. If he wins the fight, our army will serve you. If I win, your army will serve us." Goliath wore heavy armor from his head to his toes. Not only was he big, but he was also well protected.

One day a boy named David came from home to bring food to his older brothers who were in the Israelite army. David saw Goliath come out and dare the army to fight.

David told King Saul that he would fight the giant. I would have been worried, but David trusted in God.

"But you are only a boy," said King Saul.

David said, "God will help me."

David had peace. He trusted God to help him.

David went to meet Goliath without armor or a sword. He took only a sling and five stones. I'm not sure I would have been that brave. But David had put his trust in God. You and I can trust God too.

Goliath saw that David was just a boy with a sling. He tried to scare David. I would have really been worried and I might have run the other way. But not David!

He said, "You come against me with sword and spear, but I come against you in the name of the Lord Almighty, the God of the armies of Israel, whom you have defied." David was fighting this battle to show everyone that God is strong.

David took a stone and put it in the sling. Then he spun the sling over his head. The stone sailed through the air. The stone hit Goliath in the forehead where there was no armor. Goliath fell to the ground. Amazing!

David could have been too afraid to fight Goliath, but he trusted God. I want to have that kind of trust too. Don't you?

I know I can have God's peace when I trust in Him to take care of me.

Peace is a fruit of the Spirit. The Holy Spirit helps us know that God will give us peace, and that we can trust in Him to take care of our worries.

(You can keep reading in 1 Samuel to discover other ways that God took care of David.)

You Can Pray

Thank God for the example of David.
Ask God to help you learn how to trust
in Him to take care of your worries.

Detective Time

David trusted God to help him fight Goliath. God gave him peace. Connect the dots to see what David carried into battle with Goliath.

Detective Time

Circle the 16 things that are wrong in this picture. Then color the picture.

You Can Pray

Ask God to help you learn
how to trust Him more.
Thank Him for sending Jesus so that
you can know how much He loves you.

A Verse to Learn

Let the peace of Christ rule in your hearts.
(Colossians 3:15)

Colossians
3:15

God doesn't want worries to control you. He doesn't want them to make you scared, or anxious, or afraid. God wants you to trust in Him so that peace can be the ruler of your heart.

Read the verse again. Can you say it without looking at it? When you can say the whole verse without looking at it, repeat the verse for someone in your family.

When you've said the verse to someone without looking at it, circle the grasshopper on the Critter Map, page 10.

You Can Pray

Ask God for a faith that trusts in Him
when you are worried or scared.
Ask Him to give you His peace in your heart.

My Journal

What kinds of things make you worried or scared? Write about them here. Or draw a picture to show what makes you worried or scared.

You Can Pray

Talk to God about your worries. Thank Him for taking care of your worries and giving you peace.

After your prayer time, write PEACE across your list or picture of worries.

Something to Do

Make paper place mats to help you remember the story of David and Goliath. Draw pictures from the Bible story on big pieces of paper. Cover the pictures with clear Con-Tact paper. Use the pictures on the place mats to tell your family about David and Goliath.

You Can Pray

Thank God for the gift of His peace. Thank Him for His forgiveness and ask Him to help you trust in Him to take care of all your needs.

PATIENCE

A Better View

Do you know what patience is? The Bible says that patience is long-suffering. That means being willing to put up with troublesome things in your life for a long time, trusting that God will work things out.

You show patience when you take your medicine and wait for God to make you better. Or you show patience when you keep going to school even when you don't want to. Patience is trusting in God to work everything out just right.

Bunny Boo-Boo

If you spend much time in the desert, you will see cottontail rabbits. Do you know why they're called cottontails? Their tails look like fuzzy, white cotton balls.

I see these bunnies almost every day, especially in the springtime. They hop across the road and stand like statues under a tree. They bounce over the rocks in my front yard and nibble on the mesquite bushes around my house.

Cottontail bunnies also like to munch on the grass and weeds in my backyard. But the holes in my chain-link fence are too small for them to squeeze through. How do you think they get into my yard?

My furry cottontail friends dig holes under my fence so they can come in and explore my yard. I don't mind their holes under my fence because I like having bunnies come for a visit.

Every spring the cottontail rabbits have lots of babies. The baby bunnies like to nibble on our grass too.

One day I noticed a baby bunny in my yard. He was by himself and hopped on only three feet. He held his fourth foot in the air as if he had a thorn in it.

The bunny with the boo-boo snacked on weeds. Then he took a short hop on three feet. Every time he tried to hop, he'd have to stop. Then his tongue would mop the sore foot.

After the bunny gave himself about five foot baths, he was bouncing on all four feet again. The thorn had come out of his foot. The bunny patiently waited until the thorn came out of his paw. Sometimes I have to be patient, don't you?

Maybe you've had to wait awhile before getting better when you've been sick. Maybe you've had to go to school even when you don't want to. Then you discover that you've made new friends and are learning lots of things.

God is patient too. God patiently waits for everyone to come to know what He has done for us through Jesus. He lovingly waits because He wants all people to live with Him forever in heaven.

God is really patient! I want to be patient like that. Don't you?

You Can Pray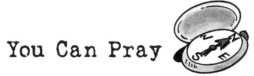

Thank God for His patience and love for everyone.
Ask Him to help you be patient in all things.

Detective Time

Draw lines between the bunnies that match. Count the matching pairs.

Detective Time

Find seven words about the bunny in our story.
The words may be written forward, backward, up, or down.

Word Bank:

- bounces
- cottontail
- digs
- explores
- furry
- hops
- nibbles

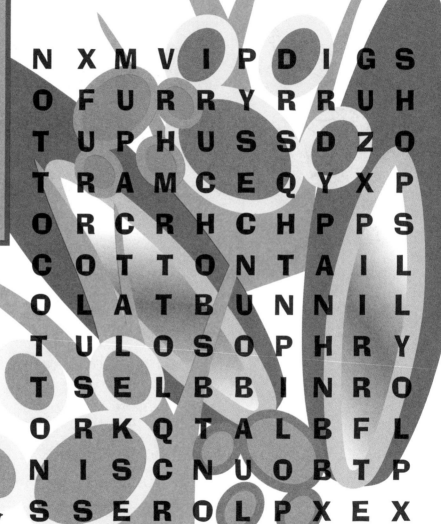

N X M V I P D I G S
O F U R R Y R R U H
T U P H U S S D Z O
T R A M C E Q Y X P
O R C R H C H P P S
C O T T O N T A I L
O L A T B U N N I L
T U L O S O P H R Y
T S E L B B I N R O
O R K Q T A L B F L
N I S C N U O B T P
S S E R O L P X E X

You Can Pray

Thank God for creating you. And thank Him for creating
bunnies, even those who get thorns in their feet.

Joshua 5:13–6:20

A Bible Story to Read

God chose Joshua to lead the Israelites into a new land. But before they could live in the Promised Land, the Israelites had to win a battle against the city of Jericho.

God told Joshua what to do to win the battle. He said, "Have the men in your army form a marching line. Have seven priests follow the army, marching in front of the ark of the covenant. Tell the priests to carry trumpets made of rams' horns. March around the city once a day for six days.

"On the seventh day, march around the city seven times.

Tell the priests to blow their trumpets. When you hear the long blast on the trumpets, have all the people give a loud shout. Then the wall of the city will fall down."

It was part of God's plan to give the city of Jericho to the people of Israel. They had waited a long time to get to the Promised Land. Now they had to wait seven more days. That took patience!

The Israelites marched around Jericho once a day for six days. After they marched around the city seven times on the seventh day, the seven priests blew the seven trumpets loud and long. The people shouted. And the walls tumbled and crumbled to the ground.

Joshua and the Israelites may not have understood why God told them to march around the city like that, but they trusted in God's plan. I want to have the kind of trust in God that teaches patience, don't you?

There may be times when we don't understand how God is working in our lives. But the Holy Spirit helps us to trust that patience will work God's will in our lives. Even when I don't understand what God is doing in my life, I want to be patient and obey Him.

 Patience is a fruit of the Spirit. The Holy Spirit helps us know that God is patient with us. Trusting in God will teach us patience.

(You can keep reading in the book of Joshua to discover what other things happened to Joshua and the Israelites.)

You Can Pray

Thank God for the example of Joshua and the Children of Israel. Ask God for a faith that will help you patiently seek His help and guidance.

Patience

God had a plan for making the walls of Jericho come down. Joshua and the Israelites had learned to trust God. Their trust gave them the patience to do what God told them to do.

Make new words out of letters in the word **PATIENCE**. Write your new words on the lines below.

NIECE
_____   _____   _____

_____   _____   _____

_____   _____   _____

_____   _____   _____

_____   _____   _____

_____   _____   _____

Detective Time

Unscramble these words about Joshua. Write the new words on the lines.

kar _____

vnenatco _____

sIelarties _____

rcJehio _____

rhcma _____

etnapice _____

sperits _____

venes _____

estmtrup _____

lawl _____

You Can Pray

Ask God to help you learn patience for Jesus' sake.
Thank Him for knowing what is best for you
even when it is hard to understand.

A Verse to Learn

As servants of God we commend ourselves ...
in purity, understanding, patience and kindness.
(2 Corinthians 6:6)

I want to be a servant of God. Don't you? We can thank Him and serve Him by being patient for Jesus' sake.

Read the verse again. Can you say the verse without looking at it? When you can say the whole verse without looking at it, tell it to someone in your family.

When you've said the verse to someone without looking at it, circle the bunny on the Critter Map, page 10.

You Can Pray

Ask God to help you be willing to serve others with patience.
Thank Him for sending Jesus.

My Journal

Patience can be very hard. Can you think of a time when you have had to trust God? Write something about patience here. Or draw a picture of a time when God helped you be patient.

You Can Pray

Thank God for always being with you and helping you, no matter what. Ask Him to help you trust in Him for patience.

Something to Do

Ask Mom or Dad to help you bake a double batch of your favorite cookies. Was it easy to wait for the cookies to bake even though you were hungry? Sometimes it is hard to show the fruit of patience. After the cookies are baked, share some with a special friend.

You Can Pray

Ask God to forgive you for the times when you have not been patient. Ask Him to help you learn how to show patience to others for Jesus' sake.

KINDNESS

A Better View

Do you know what kindness is? Someone who shows the fruit of kindness acts in a caring, generous, and thoughtful way even when it is hard to be kind to others. You show kindness when you help your little sister or brother make their bed even when they do not help. You show kindness when you share your lunch with someone even though you are still hungry.

I like it when someone shows kindness to me. I'm sure you do too. Because we sometimes sin, we need God's help to show kindness to others. He will help us learn how to be kind.

Supper Time Skunk

My husband Bob and I like to camp. One time we went camping with our friends John and Paula. They parked their motor home across the road from us.

One evening it was my turn to cook. I went across the road to our motor home to fix supper. The weather was so nice that I left the door open.

When the food was almost ready, I decided to ask Paula a question. That's when I noticed a critter on the step of our motor home, sniffing our screen door with her little black nose.

The curious critter was about the size of a cat. Her fur was black like midnight. She had a thin, white stripe down her forehead. Two white stripes ran down the middle of her back. Can you guess what kind of critter she was?

If you said a skunk, you're right! God made skunks with a special weapon to use when they think they are in danger. The skunk's weapon isn't horns like God gave bulls, or a stinger like He gave bees. Do you know what God gave skunks to protect them from their enemies?

A really smelly spray!

I didn't want our supper time skunk to think I was going to attack her. She might turn around, lift her tail, and spray. My motor home would have smelled like skunk spray for a very long time.

I didn't know what to do. I slowly backed away from the screen door. If I stayed inside to hide, supper would get cold. And if I went outside, the skunk might chase me for my supper. I quietly prayed, "What should I do, Lord?"

Then I looked out the window and saw the man who was camping next to us. I watched him hang a tote bag from a low branch on a tree. Then he tossed an orange on the ground below the bag and walked away.

The sniffing skunk strolled toward the tree. Soon it pulled oranges out of the bag and munched on them. I took our supper and hurried across the road to John and Paula's picnic table.

I was thankful for my neighbor's kindness. He was kind to give the hungry skunk a fruit snack even though he could have been sprayed by the skunk. I thanked God for that kind man who saved me and our supper from the supper time skunk.

That man's kindness reminded me of God's kindness to us. He sent Jesus to die on the cross for our sins. God is loving and kind! I want to be kind too. Don't you?

We ate our supper at the picnic table and laughed about my skunk story. The skunk wandered around the campground, sniffing the supper time smells. We didn't leave any food outside, just in case he was a midnight skunk too and decided to come back for a midnight snack.

You Can Pray

Thank God for sending Jesus to die
for the forgiveness of your sins.
Ask Him to teach you how to show
His love to others through acts of kindness.

Detective Time

The numbers 1–10 are hidden in this picture. Find each number and circle it.

Detective Time

etnt _____

suknk _____

fifingsi _____

cipinc _____

goseran _____

csrko _____

gxponreli _____

My neighbor showed kindness to me. This is a list of words about our camping trip. Can you put the letters in the right order?

You Can Pray

Thank God for creating you.
And thank Him for creating skunks—
even their smelly spray.

A Bible Story to Read

Do you remember reading about David and King Saul in the story about Goliath?

1 Samuel 20:1-42

David became very popular because he had been so brave. King Saul didn't like the attention he was getting from everyone.

King Saul wanted to be the most popular. One day he sent men to David's house to kill him, but David escaped.

King Saul had a son named Jonathan. David and Jonathan were best friends. David told Jonathan that his father was trying to kill him. Jonathan promised to help David.

I think I would have been afraid to help someone the king didn't like. But Jonathan was willing to be kind to David even if it meant he could get into trouble.

Jonathan told David to stay away until he could find out if his father really planned to kill him. The friends chose a time to meet secretly in a field where David went to hide.

Jonathan knew he could be in danger if his father found out that he was protecting David.

King Saul became angry and said to Jonathan, "You have become friends with David. As long as David is alive, you will never become king. Now send for him and bring him to me, for he must die!"

"Why should David die?" Jonathan asked.

King Saul got so angry at Jonathan that he threw his sword at him. The sword missed Jonathan, but now he knew for sure that his father wanted to kill David.

Jonathan knew it was dangerous, but he chose to show kindness to David. The two friends knew that David would not be safe unless he went away. They cried as they said good-bye. Then David left to go to a faraway place where Saul would not find him.

Jonathan was kind to David. He put David first even though he knew it would not be easy.

Jesus showed perfect kindness to everyone. He put us first when He died on the cross to save us from our sin.

I want God to use my trust in His love so my kindness can help others. Don't you?

Kindness is a fruit of the Spirit. The Holy Spirit helps us to know that God showed perfect kindness toward us through Jesus. And God will help us show kindness to others too.

(You can keep reading in 1 Samuel to find out what happened to David next.)

You Can Pray

Thank God for the example of Jonathan.
Ask God to help your faith in His loving you grow
so that you can show God's kindness to the people you meet.

Detective Time

Jonathan was kind to David. He helped keep David safe.
David hid in a field and waited for Jonathan. Follow the
numbers and connect the dots to find David.

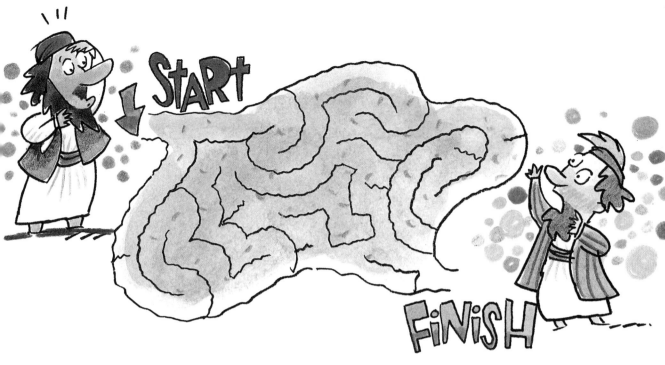

Detective Time

Jonathan and David were going to meet in secret.
Help Jonathan find David so they can say good-bye.

You Can Pray

Thank God for His kindness in sending Jesus
to be your Savior. Ask Him for a faith that will help
you put others first and show kindness to them for Jesus' sake.

Day
5

A Verse to Learn

Be kind and compassionate to one another.
(Ephesians 4:32)

God showed loving kindness to us when He sent Jesus to die for our sins. Because of what Jesus has done for us, we want to serve others in kindness.

Read the verse again. Can you say the verse without looking at it? When you can say the whole verse without looking at it, tell it to someone in your family.

When you've said the verse to someone without looking at it, circle the skunk on the Critter Map, page 10.

You Can Pray

Thank God for His kindness in creating you, providing for you, and sending a Savior for the forgiveness of your sins. Ask Him to help your faith continue to grow.

My Journal

Can you think of 10 kind things you can do for others? Write your ideas here. Or draw a picture of you doing something kind for someone in your family.

Choose one of the kind deeds from your list or your picture, and do it.

You Can Pray

Thank God that Jesus put you first when He died and rose again for your sins. Ask God to help you think of others first and share His love through kindness.

Something to Do

Use construction paper or a paper plate to make a bookmark for your best friend. Write a Bible verse, add a poem, or draw a picture. When you give the bookmark to your friend, say thank you for the gifts of kindness and friendship.

You Can Pray

Thank God for the example of others who show the fruit of their faith through kindness. Ask Him to help your faith grow so that you can show kindness to others for Jesus' sake.

GOODNESS

A Better View

What things do you call "good"? You think that a favorite food, a high grade on a test, or getting the basketball into the hoop are "good" because they make you happy. But the Bible teaches about a different type of "goodness"—the fruit of the Spirit that grows out of our trust in God's love for us.

God is perfect and everything He does for us is "good." He loves us and He wants the best for us. After all, He sent Jesus as our Savior from sin. We cannot be "good" on our own. The things we do can be called "good" only when the Holy Spirit uses us to show God's love through our words and actions.

HUMMINGBIRD SUCKER

Pastor Hutchinson was sitting on his front porch reading when he heard a funny sound. He thought he heard a little helicopter near his head. He looked up and saw an Anna's Hummingbird. The green bird buzzed over to the flower pot hanging from the roof of his porch.

The bird poked its pointy beak into one of the purple flowers. It wanted a sip of nectar, the sweet juice in flowers. Hummingbirds live on nectar. They don't eat macaroni or cookies. The sweet nectar from a flower makes a hummingbird happy.

My pastor watched as the bird buzzed from one flower to another. There was no nectar in the flowers because the flowers were plastic. They weren't real. Finally, the hummingbird gave up and left.

Sometimes we look for goodness in the wrong places. We think that things are good only if they make us happy. We forget that God is the giver of good things. We may not always understand that what God does for us is good. But, we trust that His love for us is always perfect and good.

I want the type of goodness that trusts in God's love for me. Don't you?

You Can Pray

Thank God for His goodness through
Jesus' death and resurrection.
Thank Him for the gifts of love, forgiveness,
and eternal life in heaven.

Sigh...

Detective Time

Can you count? How many hummingbirds are flying?
Write the number here.

Draw lines between the hummingbirds that match.

Detective Time

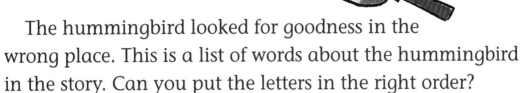

The hummingbird looked for goodness in the wrong place. This is a list of words about the hummingbird in the story. Can you put the letters in the right order?

ngeren _____

lihcotpere _____

zebuzd _____

keba _____

tencra _____

mhdrumginbi _____

tponiy _____

You Can Pray

Thank God for His goodness in creating you.
And thank Him for creating hummingbirds and flowers too.

Daniel loved God. He lived in Babylon, far away from his family. He worked hard and He was faithful to God. God blessed Daniel.

Daniel became an important man in Babylon. King Darius wanted to put him in charge of the other leaders. This made some of the leaders jealous. They decided to get rid of Daniel.

They said, "We will never find Daniel doing anything wrong. The only chance we have is to find something wrong with the law of his God." Then they came up with an evil plan.

Daniel's enemies tricked the king into signing a new law. This law said that everyone should pray only to the king. Anyone who did not pray to the king would be thrown into a den of lions.

Then they spied on Daniel. He prayed to God three times a day, kneeling in front of his window. He had heard about the new law, but he knew it was wrong to pray to anyone except God. Daniel wanted to show his love and thanks to God, even though he knew he might become lunch for some lions.

Daniel 6:1-23

He prayed to God, not King Darius.

I wouldn't have wanted to be put into a cave with a bunch of hungry lions. But Daniel trusted in God's love to protect him. He trusted in God's goodness.

The men saw Daniel praying and ran to tell the king. The king liked Daniel. He didn't want to hurt him, but King Darius knew he had to do what the law said. He told his men to throw Daniel into a den of lions.

The king said to Daniel, "May your God, whom you serve, rescue you!" Then the king's men placed a big stone over the door of the lions' den. Daniel was alone with hungry lions.

Early the next morning, King Darius went to the lions' den to check on Daniel. He called out, "Daniel, servant of the living God, has your God rescued you from the lions?"

Daniel answered, "My God sent His angel to shut the mouths of the lions. They have not hurt me."

God is so amazing! He saved Daniel! God is good to us. He has saved us from sin through Jesus. I want to share His goodness with others in my words and actions.

Goodness is a fruit of the Spirit. The Holy Spirit will help us know that God is good. We can ask Him to help us learn how to serve God and make goodness a part of our lives too.

(You can keep reading the book of Daniel to discover what happened next to Daniel.)

You Can Pray

Thank God for the example of Daniel. Ask God to help you trust in His goodness and love for Jesus' sake.

Detective Time

Connect the dots to see where Daniel is.
Will Daniel get into trouble for what he is doing? Who will help him?

Detective Time

Begin at START.
Write down the word in box
number 1. Move to the left
and write down the word you
find in every other box.
Go around the lion's mouth
twice. When you are done,
you will be able to read what
God tells us about trust. Look up
Isaiah 26:4 to check your answer.

_____ _____

_____ _____ _____,

_____ _____ _____ _____

_____ _____.

 You Can Pray

Thank God for His goodness. Ask Him to give you faith that
helps you show the love of Jesus to others.

A Verse to Learn

The LORD is good to all.
(Psalm 145:9a)

God gives us His goodness through Jesus Christ. Because of Christ, we are "good" in God's eyes. He helps us show His goodness to others through the things we say and the things that we do.

Psalm 145:9a

Read the verse again. Can you say the verse without looking at it? When you can say the whole verse without looking at it, tell it to someone in your family.

When you've said the verse to someone without looking at it, circle the hummingbird on the Critter Map, on page 10.

You Can Pray

Thank God for His goodness to you every day. Thank Him for His love and forgiveness.

 My Journal

God helps us do good things for each other. Write down some of the good things we can say and do to show God's love to others. Or draw a picture of someone doing something to show goodness.

You Can Pray

Look at the list you wrote or the picture you drew. Thank God for the people in your life who trust in God's love and show His goodness through the things they say and do.

Something to Do

Just like Daniel, I have special places where I go to read my Bible and pray at a special time each day. The swing on my porch and a rocking chair in my family room are some of those places.

Choose a special place for your daily prayer time. Decorate some pieces of paper and tie them together with string or ribbon. Make this your prayer journal and write down the things you like to talk to God about when you pray.

You Can Pray

Go to your special prayer place.
Thank God for sending Jesus for the forgiveness of your sins so that you could learn about God's goodness to you.

FAITHFULNESS

A Better View

Do you know what it means to be faithful? To be faithful means to keep a promise. Or it means being obedient and doing what you know you are supposed to do—doing what you've been taught.

Because of our sin, we might sometimes break a promise. But God is always faithful and keeps His promises perfectly. The best promise of all was sending Jesus to be our Savior.

Coyote Choir

My friend Beverly has a family
of coyotes that live behind her house.
One evening she saw two coyotes
near a clump of cottonwood trees.

The coyote is a member of
the dog family. It looks a little bit
like a small German Shepherd.
Desert coyotes are even smaller
and their fur is a lighter color.
The coyotes where I live have fur
that looks yellow and gray, with
black and brown streaks. Their bushy
tails are black at the tip. Their fuzzy ears
are pointed. And their noses are pointed too.

Coyotes are mostly nocturnal. That means they usually play
and hunt at night.

Beverly can hear the night song of coyotes. It sounds like yips
and howls. She hears howling coyotes.

God gave coyotes a special howl so they can talk to each other. They are faithful to use the yips and howls God gave them to let other coyotes know where they are.

You can usually hear other coyotes howling back if you listen closely. At night we can hear coyote choirs echo across the desert.

Beverly saw and heard the coyotes several times. She realized that they had dug a den—a coyote house—under some trees. A den is like a cave in the ground with long tunnels and many rooms.

One night Beverly heard new voices in the coyote choir that were off-key and sounded weaker. The choir had a few new and younger members. She grabbed her binoculars for a closer look at the coyote carolers.

Beverly saw two adult coyotes and five new coyote pups. Soon the baby coyotes learned how to howl as they listened to their mother and father. They also learned to howl by faithfully practicing with the voices God gave them.

Coyotes are faithful as they talk to one another. They yip and howl to keep in touch. But God is even more faithful as He speaks to us.

God speaks to us through His words in the Bible. He teaches us about forgiveness and His saving love. The Holy Spirit works faith in our hearts so that we can understand what God teaches us. God also uses people like someone in our family, a pastor, a teacher, or a friend to help teach us about Him.

I want to learn how to be faithful to God and His Word. I want to be faithful to God like He is faithful to me. Don't you?

You Can Pray

Thank God for all of the ways He is faithful in showing His love to you. Ask Him to help you hear Him speak to you through His Word.

Detective Time

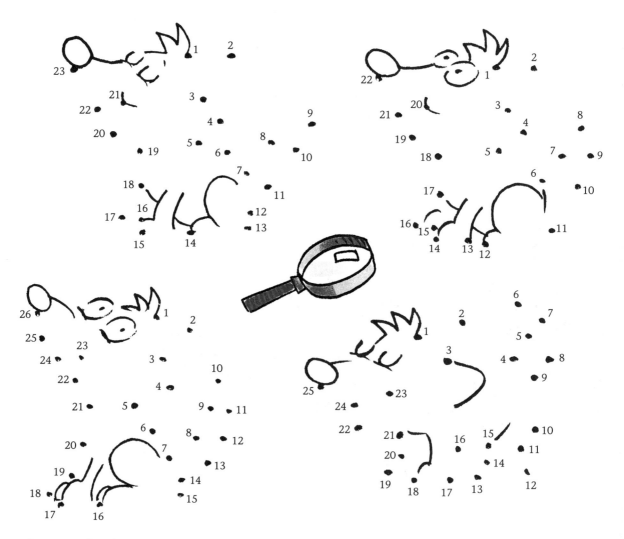

Connect the dots to see what the coyote pups are faithfully doing. Color the coyotes.

Look at the puzzle below. How many times can you find the critter's name? Look up, down, forward, and backward!

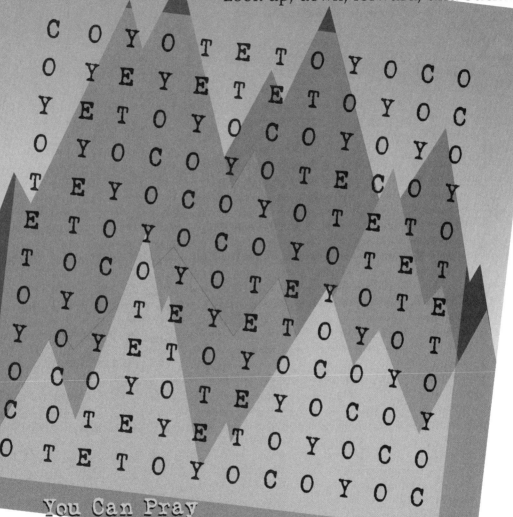

You Can Pray

Thank God for His faithfulness in creating you.
And thank Him for creating coyote choirs too.

What desert critters are faithful in joining their own choir?

_____ _____ _____ _____ _____ _____ _____.

Exodus
3:1–12

Have you heard the amazing Bible story about a man named Moses?

One day, Moses was in a field tending his sheep. He saw a bush blazing with fire. Do you know what was strange about the burning bush? It was on fire, but it wasn't turning to ashes. Amazing!

Then Moses heard God calling to him from inside the burning bush. "Moses, Moses!" God called.

"Here I am," said Moses.

"I have seen the misery of my people in Egypt," God said. "I am sending you to Pharaoh to lead My people out of Egypt."

Moses said, "Who am I to go to Pharaoh? He won't listen to me." At first it didn't seem as if Moses was going to listen to God and be faithful to obey Him.

Then God answered, "I will be with you to help you." Now Moses had God's promise.

What do you think Moses did?

He trusted God and went to Pharaoh. When Pharaoh let the Israelites go, Moses led them out of Egypt.

God may not talk to us from a burning bush, but He speaks to our hearts and minds through the Holy Spirit. God knew there would be a lot of things to make us feel alone and scared, so He sent Jesus to die on the cross and show that His perfect love is always with us. We never have to do anything without God.

I want to remember that God will always be there to help me. I want to learn how to be faithful to do what He wants me to do. Don't you?

Faithfulness is a fruit of the Spirit. The Holy Spirit helps us listen to God and learn how to be faithful to what God wants us to do.

(You can keep reading in Exodus to discover what else happens to Moses as He leads the Israelites.)

You Can Pray

Thank God for the example of Moses. Ask your heavenly Father to help you listen to His promise to love you and help you be faithful to Him for Jesus' sake.

Detective Time

Moses was faithful to listen to God and to obey Him. Think about God's faithfulness to you as you color the faces of Moses that match.

Detective Time

When God spoke to Moses from the burning bush, Moses listened. Moses was faithful when He did what God asked.

How can you be faithful to God? Unscramble the words and fill in the blanks!

ltesni   I will __ __ __ __ __ __ when I think God is speaking to me.

yobe   I will __ __ __ __ God's commands.

yrap   I will __ __ __ __ to God.

adaifr   I will not be __ __ __ __ __ __ because I know God is with me.

soprisme I will try to keep my __ __ __ __ __ __ __ __ .

rtuts   I will __ __ __ __ __ in God.

shoeco   I will __ __ __ __ __ __ to do what is right.

You Can Pray

Thank God for being faithful to His promise and sending Jesus to be your Savior. Ask God to help you be faithful and to do what He asks of you.

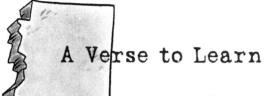

A Verse to Learn

Day
5

Obey God rather than men.
(Acts 5:29)

In this verse, the word *men* means all people. All people are sinners and only God is perfect. We need to be careful not to obey people if they tell us to do something that God does not want us to do. That would be obeying people rather than obeying God. We are faithful when we listen to what God wants us to do, even if other people do something else.

Read the verse again. Can you say the verse without looking at it? When you can say the whole verse without looking at it, tell it to someone in your family.

When you've said the verse to someone without looking at it, circle the coyote on the Critter Map, page 10.

You Can Pray

Thank God for being faithful to you.
Ask God to help you be faithful in obeying Him.

My Journal

God always keeps His promises. We can count on Him to be faithful. Write about a promise you would like God to help you keep. Or draw a picture about it.

You Can Pray

Thank God for keeping His promises, especially His promise to send a Savior. Ask Him to help you be faithful too.

Something to Do

Use paper bags and crayons to make paper bag puppets. Make a Moses puppet, a Pharaoh puppet, and a puppet of the burning bush. Use your puppets to tell the Bible story to your family and friends.

You Can Pray

Thank God for His faithfulness to you.
Ask Him for a faith that will show your faithfulness to Him.

GENTLENESS

Day 1

A Better View

Do you know what gentleness is? Gentleness means treating others in a way that makes them feel special. You treat others with gentleness when you make them feel as if they are more important to you than you are to yourself.

Proverbs 15:1 says, *"A gentle answer turns away wrath, but a harsh word stirs up anger."* Harsh words are not gentle. They are unkind or mean. Words like these make others angry, but gentle or kind words help others stay calm. By ourselves, we cannot show gentleness. The Holy Spirit helps us learn about gentleness for Jesus' sake.

Sidewalk Sparrow

April is usually sunny and warm in the desert. Once we had a surprise on April 1. It began to snow. It snowed for four days at my house. I think the birds were surprised too.

Many different kinds of birds live in the desert. Sparrows are one kind of flying critter we have in the desert. They are common birds everywhere. You can probably see sparrows even where you live.

During our big April storm, my husband Bob found a baby sparrow. It was lying on the sidewalk at the hospital where he works. The bird was cold and sick. It didn't move when he picked it up.

Bob is not a people doctor, or a critter doctor. He helps keep the computers working at the hospital. I guess that makes him a computer doctor. Still, Bob knew the sick sparrow needed a gentle touch and some tender care.

Cradling the cold bird in his hand, Bob took it to his office. He gently rubbed its frozen feathers. He used his body heat to give the bird some warmth.

Soon, after being inside the warm building and feeling Bob's body heat, the bird opened its eyes. Bob felt its breath on his hand. He knew the critter was getting stronger.

After about an hour in the warmth of Bob's hand, the baby sparrow began chirping. One of the nurses who works at the hospital took the bird home with her. She cared for it until the sparrow was strong enough to fly away.

Bob's gentle care of that baby bird reminded me of the way God cares for us. God showed us gentleness when He put us first, sending His own Son to die on the cross for our sins. He surrounds us with gentleness every day.

Sometimes I feel like God is holding me in the palm of His hand, just like Bob cradled that cold baby sparrow in his hand.

God's gentleness is everywhere. I want God to help me be gentle too. Don't you?

You Can Pray

Thank God for putting you first and sending Jesus as your Savior. Thank Him for the loving way that He cares for you, making you feel special as His child.

Day 2

Detective Time

Bob's gentle care of the baby sparrow helped
to make it well again. Connect the dots to see what
the bird is doing now.

Detective Time

Use the words in the Word Bank to complete this puzzle.

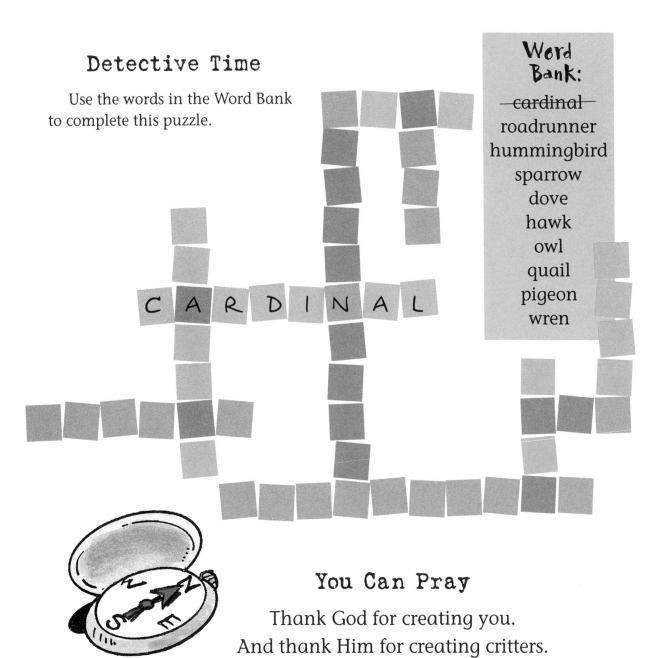

C A R D I N A L

You Can Pray

Thank God for creating you.
And thank Him for creating critters.

Esther
2:17–7:10

Esther and her cousin Mordecai were Jewish. King Xerxes made Esther the queen of Persia when she was very young.

King Xerxes made Haman his top leader. The king gave the order that everyone was to honor Haman by kneeling before him. Everyone bowed to Haman, except for Mordecai. He would only worship and bow down before the one true God.

Haman was angry with Mordecai. He came up with an evil plan to hurt him and the Jewish people. Haman went to the king and said, "The Jewish people are different than the rest of us and they do not obey the king's laws. If it pleases the king, let a new law be made to destroy them."

(Haman was not a gentle man. He let his pride and his anger control him.)

King Xerxes said, "Do what you want with these people."

Mordecai heard about Haman's plan to destroy the Jewish people. He went to Queen Esther for help. He asked her to go before the king and beg for kindness for her people.

The king didn't know that Esther was Jewish. But now her cousin Mordecai and her people were going to be killed. What would Esther do?

Sometimes we are not gentle when someone tries to hurt us or someone we love. We might get angry and even want to hurt them back. But the Bible says that Esther did not get angry. She prayed for three days and asked God what she should do. That's gentleness!

Esther put on her royal robes and went before the king. King Xerxes was pleased. "What would you like?" he asked. Esther asked the king and Haman to come to a special banquet.

While they were at the banquet, King Xerxes asked, "What would you like?" The king wanted to give Queen Esther whatever she asked for.

She made her request in a gentle manner. "If it pleases you, O king, please give me my life and spare the lives of my people. They are going to be destroyed."

"Where is the man who has dared to do such a thing?" asked the king.

Esther answered, "The man who is trying to hurt us is Haman."

King Xerxes punished Haman for tricking him into signing the order to kill the Jewish people.

Esther and her people were safe again. The king gave Queen Esther all of Haman's property. Then King Xerxes made Mordecai his top leader.

God used Esther's gentleness to save His people. I want God to use me to do His work too. Don't you?

Gentleness is a fruit of the Spirit. The Holy Spirit helps us know that God is gentle. He helps us learn how to show gentleness to others.

(You can keep reading in the book of Esther to discover what else happened to Esther and Mordecai.)

You Can Pray

Thank God for the example of Esther. Ask Him to help you learn how to serve others by treating them with gentleness.

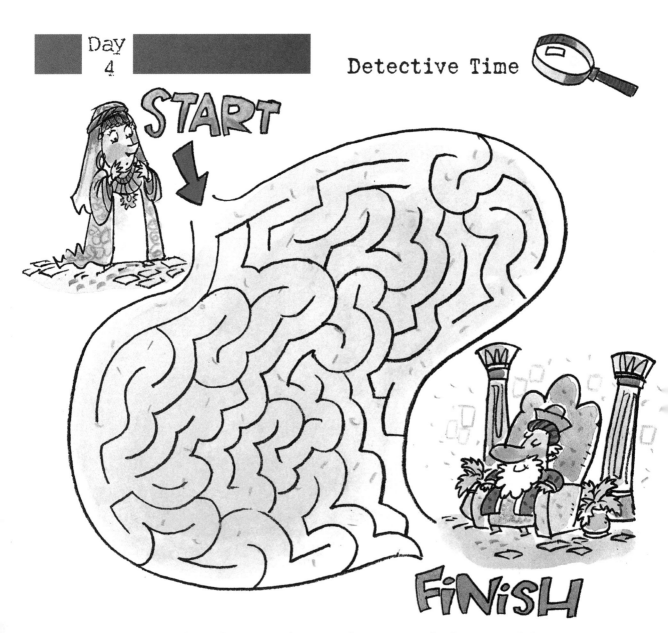

START

FINISH

Esther showed gentleness in the way she went to the king to ask him to save her people. Help Esther find her way to the king's inner court.

Detective Time

A	B	C	D	E	F	G	H	I	J	K	L	M
1	2	3	4	5	6	7	8	9	10	11	12	13

N	O	P	Q	R	S	T	U	V	W	X	Y	Z
14	15	16	17	18	19	20	21	22	23	24	25	26

___ ___ ___ ___ ___ ___
5   19 20 8   5   18

___ ___ ___ ___ ___ ___
24 5   18 24 5   19

___ ___ ___ ___ ___
8   1   13 1   14

___ ___ ___ ___ ___ ___ ___ ___
13 15 18 4   5   3   1   9

Use the code to write the names of the people in the Bible story.

You Can Pray

Ask God to forgive you for the times you are not gentle.
Ask for His help in learning how to show gentleness to others.

A Verse to Learn

Let your gentleness
be evident to all.
The Lord is near.
(Philippians 4:5)

The word *evident* means to make something easy to see. God wants others to be able to see the gentleness the Holy Spirit helps us to have. Your gentleness will be seen by others as they watch what you do and listen to what you say.

Read the verse again. Can you say the verse without looking at it? When you can say the whole verse without looking at it, tell it to someone in your family.

When you have said the verse to someone without looking at it, circle the sparrow on the Critter Map, page 10.

You Can Pray

Thank God for being with you.
Ask Him to help you think about ways to show gentleness in the things you do and the things you say.

My Journal

What do you think is best about being gentle instead of getting mad? Write it down. Or draw a picture about it.

You Can Pray

Think about people who show gentleness to you.
Thank God for these gentle people in your life.

Something to Do

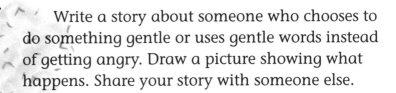

Write a story about someone who chooses to do something gentle or uses gentle words instead of getting angry. Draw a picture showing what happens. Share your story with someone else.

You Can Pray

Thank God for His gentleness.
Ask Him to help you choose gentleness instead of anger and other things that hurt others. Thank Him for His gift of forgiveness through Jesus.

SELF-CONTROL

A Better View

Do you know what self-control is? Self-control is choosing to do the right thing, even when you want to do something else. You show self-control when you choose not to yell at your sister or brother. Or when you don't take something that does not belong to you. Self-control is also telling the truth when you feel like lying.

We are sinners and we cannot have self-control by ourselves. But God sent Jesus as the Savior to forgive our sins. He also gives us faith that will help us show self-control and choose to do what is right.

Pack Rat Surprise

Chris is married to our daughter Amy. One weekend Chris and Amy came over. While they were there, Chris and Bob moved the old woodpile that was sitting outside our fence.

They loaded the wood into a wheelbarrow. Suddenly, a big, brown, ball of fur popped out of the pile and scurried away. Chris jumped back so fast that he almost fell on the ground.

Chris had grown up in East Africa. He was used to seeing lots of critters—like baboons and warthogs. But he wasn't too crazy about this critter. It had a long skinny tail, a pointy nose, and whiskers. Can you guess what it was?

If you said it was a rat, you were right. The pack rat had built a nest at the bottom of our woodpile. Do you know why the white-throated wood rat is called a pack rat?

The rat had packed lots of things in its nest. Bob found mesquite bean pods, an empty can, pieces of newspaper, pink ribbon, and a green tennis ball.

Wood rats don't have much self-control. When they see something they like, they just take it and pack it into their nest. Sometimes we are just like the pack rat. We want everything we see.

In Philippians 4:11, the Apostle Paul writes, *"I have learned to be content."* To be content means to be happy or pleased with whatever you have. Paul had learned to be happy with what he had because he trusted God to take care of him.

When we use God's help to focus on His friendship with us for Jesus' sake, we can be content with what we have. He will help us be content instead of focusing on other things we might want. God will give us the faith to help us exercise self-control.

I want a faith that will help me exercise self-control. Don't you? I want to be happy with what I have, instead of always wanting more.

You Can Pray

Thank God for the many things
He has given to you,
especially His gift of forgiveness
through Jesus. Ask Him to help you
be content with what you have.

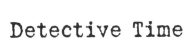

Detective Time

A pack rat doesn't show self-control, does it?
This pack rat wants more and more
things for his pile.

The numbers 1 to 10 are hidden in this picture. Find each number and circle it.

Detective Time

The desert is where all of the critters live that we have discovered in our stories. Can you build off the word *desert* and spell out the words in the Word Bank?

Word Bank:

~~desert~~
grasshopper
hummingbird
quail
rabbit
lizard
pack rat
roadrunner
skunk
sparrow

D E S E R T

You Can Pray

Thank God for creating you.
And thank Him for creating critters.

Bible Story to Read

Genesis 27:5–43

Jacob and Esau were twins, but Esau was born first.

Their father Isaac had grown old. One day Isaac called for his oldest son Esau. He said, "Go hunting for some meat. Prepare it the way I like. Then bring it to me to eat so that I may give you my blessing before I die." Esau left to go hunting.

Jacob and Esau's mother heard this. She wanted Jacob to get the special blessing instead of Esau. She and Jacob planned to trick Isaac.

Jacob's mother cooked two goats so Jacob could give Isaac some tasty food. She put goat hair on Jacob's hands and neck so Isaac would think that Jacob was Esau. Then Jacob put on some of his brother's clothes. He pretended to be Esau and took the food to his father.

Isaac asked, "Who is it?"

"I am Esau," said Jacob. (He chose to lie to get what He wanted. Jacob didn't use self-control.)

Isaac thought it was Esau bringing him food. So he gave the blessing. Jacob's trick had worked.

If Jacob had used self-control, he would have been happy to ask for his own blessing. He wouldn't have lied about being Esau. Getting what he wanted was more important to Jacob than pleasing God.

Esau and his father were very angry when they found out about Jacob's trick. The sins of this family caused many problems. Our sins cause many problems in our lives. But God's loving self-control leads Him to forgive our sins for Jesus' sake. Our trust in God's love leads us to depend on Him instead of listening to others. The Holy Spirit helps us to be content with God's love and to do things that show our trust in Him.

I want a faith that shows contentment and self-control. Don't you?

Self-control is a fruit of the Spirit.
The Holy Spirit helps us learn to
make the right choices. He helps
us listen to what pleases God.
With His help we can be content
and learn to exercise self-control.

(You can keep reading in Genesis to learn more about Jacob and Esau.)

You Can Pray

Thank God for loving you. Ask Him for a faith
that trusts in His love and leads you
to depend on Him for Jesus' sake.

Detective Time

Jacob and his family did not use self-control. Connect the dots to see who helped Jacob trick his father and steal his brother's blessing.

Detective Time

Unscramble these words about Jacob and Esau. Write them on the lines below.

rorstbhe _____

afreht _____

romeht _____

slesnbig _____

kitcr _____

yhiar _____

selat _____

eil _____

You Can Pray

Ask God to give you a faith that shows self-control. Ask Him to forgive you for the times you choose to do the wrong things.

A Verse to Learn

I have learned to be content whatever the circumstances.
(Philippians 4:11)

The word *circumstance* can mean a place or a situation. Paul tells us that God helped him learn to be happy wherever He was and with whatever God gave him. Are you content with what you have?

Read the verse again. Can you say the verse without looking at it? When you can say the whole verse without looking at it, tell it to someone in your family.

When you've said the verse to someone without looking at it, circle the pack rat on the Critter Map, page 10.

You Can Pray

Thank God for the things He has given you, especially for the gift of Jesus, your Savior.
Ask Him for a faith that will help you choose to say and do things that will show your love and thanks to Him.

My Journal

Make a list of things you are thankful for.
Or draw a picture about some of these things.

You Can Pray

Thank God for sending Jesus as your Savior.
Ask Him to forgive your sins and help you learn
how to exercise self-control in your life.

Day 7 — Something to Do

Make a poster. Find a large piece of construction paper or poster board. Use colored markers to write SELF-CONTROL on the poster. Add stickers and pictures from magazines that show people showing their love or being kind. (Be sure to ask permission before cutting pictures out of magazines.)

Hang your poster where you will see it every day. Let it help you remember to show love and to choose to do the best thing.

You Can Pray

Thank God for being a loving God.
Ask Him to help you learn self-control and to
help you be happy with all of His good gifts for you.

Puzzle Answers

Page 17: 10 quail

Page 18: quail, mesquite, rabbits, sagebrush, hawk, raven, cactus

Page 23: Love the LORD your God with all your heart and with all your soul and with all your strength.

Page 31: 26 times

Page 32: reptiles, scales, bugs, cold-blooded, warm, desert, push-ups

Page 38: A cheerful heart is good medicine, but a crushed spirit dries up the bones.

Page 37:

```
N  G  N  I  S  X
E  K  I  N  G  S
H  I  A  S  E  E
M  K  Y  T  S  T
H  L  R  R  B  I
R  A  P  U  C  L
L  W  U  M  I  E
G  A  T  E  S  A
A  L  P  N  C  R
T  L  E  T  S  S
S  K  X  S  P  I
P  R  A  Y  E  R
```

Page 48:

```
S  X  C  R  I  C  K  E  T  S
R  B  S  Y  N  B  Z  T  A  R
E  U  S  M  S  S  S  G  R  U
P  G  N  A  T  S  T  N  A  G
P  S  O  L  I  V  E  T  N  A
O  C  I  R  C  R  K  A  T  T
H  O  P  P  K  R  C  N  U  S
S  L  R  K  B  X  R  N  L  T
S  T  O  C  U  T  C  T  A  I
A  B  C  I  G  U  B  R  S  C
R  E  S  T  S  T  I  C  M  K
G  R  S  S  H  P  P  R  S  S
```

Page 63:

```
N  X  M  V  I  P  D  I  G  S
O  F  U  R  R  Y  R  R  U  H
T  U  P  H  U  S  S  D  Z  O
T  R  A  M  C  E  Q  Y  X  P
O  R  C  R  H  C  H  P  P  S
C  O  T  T  O  N  T  A  I  L
O  L  A  T  B  U  N  N  I  L
T  U  L  O  S  O  P  H  R  Y
T  S  E  L  B  B  I  N  R  O
O  R  K  Q  T  A  L  B  F  L
N  I  S  C  N  U  O  B  T  P
S  S  E  R  O  L  P  X  E  X
```

143

Page 68: ark, covenant, Israelites, Jericho, march, patience, priests, seven, trumpets, wall

Page 78: tent, skunk, sniffing, picnic, oranges, rocks, exploring

Page 91: green, helicopter, buzzed, beak, nectar, hummingbird, pointy

Page 96: Trust in the LORD forever for the LORD is the Rock eternal.

Page 105: 28 times

Page 110: listen, obey, pray, afraid, promises, trust, choose

Page 125: Esther, Xerxes, Haman, Mordicai

Page 139: brothers, father, mother, blessing, trick, hairy, steal, lie

Page 119:

Page 134: